May I Hate God?

by
Pierre Wolff

PAULIST PRESS
New York/Ramsey/Toronto

Scripture quotations are taken from *The Jerusalem Bible* copyright © 1966 by Darton, Longman & Todd Ltd. and Doubleday and Company.

Imprimi Potest
Richard T. Cleary, S.J.
April 27, 1978

Library of Congress
Catalog Card Number: 78-70815

ISBN: 0-8091-2180-8

Published by Paulist Press
Editorial Office: 1865 Broadway, New York, N.Y. 10023
Business Office: 545 Island Road, Ramsey, N.J. 07446

Printed and bound in the
United States of America

Contents

To Henri,
Marie-Therese,
to all who have helped me,
and to all who have shared with me
their agony,
thank you.

Foreword

For anyone who is seriously interested in developing a spiritual life, this is an important book. It is a small book, but one that can open large areas of our soul to the loving touch of God. It is written by a man who has guided many men and women in their spiritual journeys and has acquired keen insight into the fears, hesitations, and inhibitions that prevent us from tasting and seeing the goodness of the Lord.

I count myself among the happy group who experienced Pierre Wolff's careful guidance during a thirty day retreat and an eight day follow-up retreat here in the United States. I can therefore say with great conviction that what Pierre Wolff has written is less the result of reading books than of reading human souls. I myself have experienced what he describes here, and I am very glad that through this book his guidance will no longer be limited to those he can reach in directed retreats.

The main question of this book, "May I hate God?", touches the very center of our spiritual struggle. I would not be surprised if hostility, anger, resentment, and hatred proved to be the greatest stumbling blocks to our spiritual growth. Especially when we strongly desire to experience God's presence in our lives and to taste love, joy, and peace as

1

its fruits, the awareness of hateful feelings often startles and confuses us so much that we hide ourselves from him whom we are seeking.

In a very revealing way, Pierre Wolff shows how the anger and hatred which separate us from God can become the doorway to greater intimacy with him. We have been so victimized by religious and secular taboos against anger and hatred that these emotions usually evoke only shame and guilt. Seldom, if ever, are they expressed in a creative way. But Scripture presents us with a real alternative. In both the Old and New Testaments, it is clear that only by expressing our anger and hatred directly to God will we come to know the fullness of both his love and our freedom.

This is a very timely book. In a world full of violence, destruction, conflicts, and wars, feelings of anger and hatred are quickly drawn to the surface of our consciousness. Our first response to such feelings is to hide them from God in the belief that they have no place in our spiritual life. In so doing, however, we limit our relationship with him to pious moments or sentimental hours. Our spiritual life then loses strength and power and quickly becomes divorced from the issues that really matter.

Pierre Wolff shows us how we can do real harm to ourselves when we approach God selectively and reveal to him only those parts of ourselves that we think he can handle. He reclaims the biblical tradition in which God is confronted with the pains of the world, directly exposed to our anger and hatred, and challenged to show us that he really cares.

Pierre Wolff thus offers us a way to make our prayer stronger and deeper, more realistic, and more intimate.

The two appendices add to the practical usefulness of the book. The first offers concrete suggestions for those who direct retreats, and the second contains a wealth of scriptural references for use in meditation when anger and hatred begin to dominate our feelings. There are texts for times when we feel betrayed and ill-treated and for times when we are angry at God and doubt his faithfulness and love. There are texts for use in times of trial and texts that give us words with which to ask for grace and healing. In this small book, therefore, Pierre Wolff not only guides our spiritual life in a new direction, but also offers us concrete "exercises" to help us walk this new road.

I hope and pray that many people will come across this little book and take an hour of their time to read it. I am sure that for those who, like me, have known anger and hatred in their lives, the following pages will open new horizons and will mark the beginning of a new, very honest encounter with the Lord.

Henri J. M. Nouwen

THE OTHER HALF OF THE COVENANT:
A LAYMAN'S DECALOGUE TO GOD

Thou shalt love man as much as man loves thee.
Thou shalt honor thy promise to Noah.
Thou shalt protect all children from every natural
   harm.
Thou shalt ease childbirth's travail.
Thou shalt match man's pace toward peace.
Thou shalt not cause the birth of crippled children.
Thou shalt not steal children from their parents.
Thou shalt not cause the poor, the innocent or the
   faithful to suffer famine.
Thou shalt not harden any man's heart.
Thou shalt not test one man more than any other
   man.
Amen.

—An American Prisoner

Introduction

To those who suffer.
To those who will suffer someday.

The title of this book may come as a surprise to people who think that such a question has no place in a believer's life. Some will see the title as blasphemy, even though it is followed by a question mark. Others will see no point to such a question.

These reactions may be justified, but they come up against an undeniable reality: even though they are believers, many men and women overwhelmed by suffering not only ask the question within themselves but actually begin to hate their God.

When I look at the experiences of some friends of mine, I understand: Being widowed at the age of twenty-six with three children to raise because my husband was killed in a senseless war just before he was to return home. Seeing my family life destroyed because my parents are alcoholics. Losing my baby when he fell from a fifth-floor window. Suffering total ruin after years of working and saving because a dam broke and flood waters destroyed everything.

Becoming severely handicapped in an automobile accident because the other driver was intoxicated. Being fired and then unemployed for years because my employer went bankrupt through lack of intelligent management and desire for selfish profit. Feeling the pain of poverty day after day in a developing country exploited by foreign businessmen allied with my country's own leaders.

I understand that people like these can look at God and begin to say, "Hey, wait a minute...Why?...Why me?...Why this?

Every day in thousands of hearts realities like these create revolt, resentment and sometimes hatred of the Lord, by whatever name he may be called. This is a fact that carries more weight than the question on the cover of this book.

For you who are faced with such reality I wrote this book.

It was written first of all for you.

May it help you as it has helped people I know—the people who taught me what this book contains. It was written by suffering people for other suffering people. I am lending my voice, but the book is theirs.

May its consolation become yours and help you.

You who have not yet really suffered, please remember the message of these pages. Remember first of all so that you can deal more gently with persons who suffer. But also remember so that you

6

will be able to face your own grief when it comes into your heart. No one can escape such an experience; that is why I can prophesy that you will need these words.

May they be in your memory when winter enters your life.

I realize that this book is written with mere words, words which are often powerless in the face of adversity. But to the extent that words can reach out to touch someone whose heart is torn in pieces, I offer them in the hope that they will.

Communicating with Another

When we suffer we desire either to remain silent or to talk with someone. I will speak later about silence. Let me first deal with the problem we face when we want to communicate with someone else.

Suffering makes us realize how essential it is to communicate. Without communication we can have no real relationship with anyone. Without communication the other does not exist for me, nor do I exist for the other. Only when we begin to communicate do we exist for each other. A person who is suffering wants to exist for other people.

There is no neutrality in communicating: if I have a bond with someone, each of us means something for the other. If neutrality enters into my communication with someone, communication quickly comes to an end. When we are suffering we know how difficult it is to deal with people who are not interested in us; their indifference kills both communication and relationship. We feel that we do not exist for them—and neither does our main concern, our sorrow.

Communication always implies a certain affective "charge" between the persons concerned. This is true even when it does not appear clearly. Two strangers in an elevator are really communicating, so much so that as soon as one of them gets too close to the other, the latter feels uneasy. Two businessmen bargaining with characteristic coolness invest their own interests in the contract and therefore communicate through their affectivity. This affective "charge" is even more prominent in a communication attempted by one who is suffering.

Communication cannot be reduced to words. We often think it takes place only in phrases and sentences. But other things can also touch us deeply: a letter; a hand shaking ours in silence; a closed fist. A gift, sent or received, means so much; so does a caress, a sign of tenderness. So although I shall speak essentially about verbal signs, or words, I do not want to oversimplify the meaning of communication.

I remember a retreatant tied in knots and a sister with cancer, both unable to communicate. Both began their "dialogue" with me in the same way: they held out their hands and extended their fingers in a gesture of openness and offering. In silence communication began.

Similarly, I remember a woman: The child she was watching fell from the window and was crushed to death five floors below. And another woman: Her four-year-old daughter succumbed to a brain tumor. In both cases we came with friends to embrace these heartbroken women, simply holding their hands in ours during a long, a very long, silence.

Let us now examine the strongest feeling we can deal with—*hatred*.

10

Hatred

Strangely enough, people do not always recognize hatred as a form of communication. They too easily believe that communication means a positive bond, a warm attraction. Yet, because they hate someone, these same people cannot sleep for weeks, become easily irritated, think up countless ways to get justification or revenge and cannot cope with their everyday occupations. Whether they like it or not, they are totally preoccupied with the object of their hate. Their whole life is focused on him or her, more intensely perhaps than if they loved the person.

No one absorbs us more than the person we hate. Remember when you hated someone?

And yet, two men wrestling with each other are very close.

We are sometimes told that love can blind us. How much more true is this of hatred! It is next to impossible to fight hatred with reason; it is always difficult to be reasonable when we are filled with hate. All our doors are locked. Our consciousness is narrowed to the size of the shortsightedness of our hatred.

The bitterness of hatred is so great that it seizes

11

our existence and develops in us a boundless power and violence rarely shown in other circumstances. Some politicians who know this strength use it for their own purposes in dealing with the masses. Anyone who has seen a crowd possessed by hatred can attest to its power.

The power and the violence of hatred are displayed in many ways. For instance, the one we hate may loom so large in our life that we are constantly threatened by him, either in reality or in imagination. Hatred creates obsession, and it is impossible to remove it from our mind and heart.

Hatred is an enduring feeling. Hatred that lasts for years and years is all around us; it may even be in us.

In 1948 I was on vacation at my grandmother's house in a small village. One day I went to buy tobacco in the only store that carried it. When I returned, my grandmother reproached me for going near *those* people who hated her and whom she hated since 1904! I had a hard time explaining my refusal to be a part of this hatred whose reasons were not at all clear to me. And the so-called "reasons" sounded rather suspicious.

This internal hatred can reach such a point that it has only one goal: to eliminate the one who is hated, perhaps by murder. Hatred is so tenacious, however, that it can continue after the death of one done away with. Anyone who has met a person who murdered through hatred can attest to this fact. It seems that killing did not remove the obsession; therefore the hated one remains "alive."

Is it then possible to deny that hatred is a kind of communication that creates strong bonds between two people?

To list all the reasons we could find for hatred within ourselves would be impossible. I may have undergone an injustice, violence to my person, or suffered an unjustified rejection—or I feel that I did. One thing that gives rise to hatred is the reversal of love or friendship. My love may have been deeply disappointed, scoffed at, rejected, hurt, in a way I could not accept; I begin to hate the one responsible. We can see in this case how hatred remains communication: The affective "charge" between two persons remains; only its quality is changed.

Through hatred the other continues to exist for us. The real way of "killing" someone, of eliminating or reducing him or her to nothing in our life is to be indifferent. Indifference really kills, for then people have no reality at all for us. Hatred sometimes reaches this level. But as long as hatred is still operative in communication and relationship, it is still something, and therefore not hopeless. Proof of this can be found in soldiers whose nations were wartime enemies; when the wounds had healed, they became partners in a common effort. Let us remember the American Civil War.

Can I Be Freed from Hating?

In our friendships and our loves we have known times when revolt, anger, disappointment and resentment appeared, feelings which devoured us like a cancer. If they persisted for a long time, we risked having our injured love explode into hatred.

The only means of overcoming this risk is to express feelings of hatred openly.

Expressing Feelings of Hatred

A wife finds relief in talking with a friend about the resentment she feels against her husband. If the friend is patient in listening to her, she will be helped. But is this enough? Not usually, because the person concerned—the husband—is not yet involved.

I remember one such case, where three of us spent the afternoon together: husband, wife and myself. For months I had listened to each one separately. Finally they were telling each other all that had been building up over two years. What a confrontation...but it opened the abscess, washed away suspicion, cleared up misunderstanding. By the end of that day, we all had headaches, but the couple set out on a new path with hope in their hearts.

15

The key is to be able to express resentment to the one who caused it. When a husband *can* express his anger to his wife, when a person *can* express his revolt to his friend, healing is probably at hand. Why?

Primarily because the pus comes out of the abscess, allowing the inflammation and infection to heal.

Essentially because expression of this kind presupposes an exceptional love between the spouses or the friends. ("Presupposes" does not mean guarantees, however; that is why I underlined the word "can.")

It is taken for granted that the person who expresses himself in such a manner believes firmly that the love, the friendship, of the other can accept and welcome the words which are spoken, the feelings which burn, without judgment or criticism. When I can freely show anger to my friend, I also show, paradoxically, that I believe his love is able to take it. If I cannot be myself with my friend, exactly as I am right now, for better or for worse, with whom can I be myself? Beneath my anger my behavior says this: At least with you I can reveal myself as I am.

It is also taken for granted that my friend discerns that the root of my feelings is the love which was injured, or which I thought was injured: A love as deep as my violence is great; a love crying out its inability to live divided and its desire for reconciliation in justice.

Six years of marriage were followed by six years of extra-marital affairs for one husband and wife. One evening they decided to tell each other the truth, holding back nothing. The painful but frank confrontation ended on a note of challenge: let's begin again. Six years later, after her husband's death in an automobile accident, the widow confided to me, "These past six years were the most beautiful of our life, of our love."

Great love underlies the risk of such an encounter. Of course we must take the risk intelligently, choosing the opportune moment, the fitting place, the right tone of voice. An abscess must be lanced at the proper time. So it is usually a good idea to reflect and to pray for a while in order to calm our superficial feelings, our immediate reactions. But the risk we take is proportionate to the love we believe is there. We risk everything because we believe this love is strong enough to save everything. The confrontation will probably be a fiery one, burning but also cauterizing. A fire like this will do more good than talking with any number of friends who do not really understand.

Our Companion: Job

Now we are ready to encounter the man who symbolizes in the scriptures the experience we know when we suffer: Job.

Blessed be the Lord for Job's book!

Poor Job.

His friends, alas, understand everything and explain it all so easily. Like certain spiritual people, they rush to save his soul, judging and condemning with a sureness that even God will not show. And worst of all, they are convinced that they speak in the name of Yahweh. I am summing up their actions quickly, as I do not wish to spend any more time with them.

It is important, though, to take note of how they act, because when we come face to face with someone in pain and anger we can be this kind of "friend." We have all had to deal with such "friends" in times of personal sorrow. As if it were possible to understand or judge the feelings of someone who is torn apart with grief!

As a matter of fact, of course, it is easy for us to judge, to advise, to explain, to offer consolation, when we ourselves are not suffering. But once we have known personally or through someone we love the hard realities of birth control or unemployment, or abortion or enslavement, or homosexuality or cancer, sterility or death, it is no longer so simple.

Job himself says to his friends:

I too could talk like you,
were your soul in the plight of mine.
I too could overwhelm you with sermons,
I could shake my head over you,
and speak words of encouragement,
until my lips grew tired. (16:4-5)

Let us even suppose that the one who rebels is really guilty. May God grant that we remember how easy it is for us to speak when we are not involved; may he invite us to greater reserve and discretion. We do not have to justify the other—and he often knows that his behavior cannot be justified. What we have to do is understand him. To sympathize does not mean to agree with. But compassion always demands communion.

Consider one of my friends recounting her calvary through abortion. Or another friend confiding his shame and sense of failure because of his homosexuality. Things were clear between us from the start—but these people were crushed. I tried to be there, in silence, with my love.

The hospital chaplain stood there, the picture of health, towering over the old man obsessed with fear of damnation. He said to him, "Don't worry, it's nothing. It will go away. Make an effort to receive communion tomorrow; it will do you good." After he left, I could only sit down beside the man, take his hand and murmur, "It's not easy, this anguish..." and remain there in silence.

Job's friends do not realize that all they have to do is to be present in silence. "I wish someone would teach you to be quiet—the only wisdom that becomes you!" says Job (13:5). But no; they go on for pages and pages until we are exhausted by them and their discourses.

We are not only tired, but ill at ease and irritated. No doubt this is because we sense a certain *disdain* in their attitudes. Aren't they in fact looking down on Job, taking too lightly the weight of his sorrow and of the events which have wounded him, with all their explanations, consolations and judgments? Or do we sense that they *fear* confronting the anguish provoked by Job's questions in anyone willing to admit them? Let us try to pray with the prisoner's prayer at the beginning of this book; we may perhaps feel this anguish.

In short their flood of words tires us and exasperates us. We probably feel what Job felt—what God himself felt. For Yahweh says to Eliphaz of Teman, "I burn with anger against you and your two friends for not speaking truthfully about me as my servant Job has done" (42:7).

Job Expresses His Anger

Let us turn now to Job. What terrible things he is saying to the Lord. We cannot call them hate, but

21

we certainly must recognize the violence of Job's expressions. He does not treat the Lord with kid gloves. Let us examine some of his harshest phrases in order to realize what we in our turn might dare to say.

May the day perish when I was born,
and the night that told of a boy conceived.
May that day be darkness,
may God on high have no thought for it,
may no light shine on it.
May murk and shadow claim it for their own,
clouds hang over it,
eclipse swoop down on it. (3:3-5)

Why did I not die new-born,
not perish as I left the womb?
Why were there two knees to receive me,
two breasts for me to suck?
Had there not been, I should now be lying in
    peace,
wrapped in a restful slumber...
or put away like a still-born child that never
    came to be,
like unborn babes that never see the light.
    (3:11-13, 16)

Why give light to a man of grief?
Why give life to those bitter of heart,
who long for a death that never comes,
and hunt for it more than for a buried
    treasure?...

Why make this gift of light to a man who
    does not see his way,
whom God baulks on every side?...
For me there is no calm, no peace;
my torments banish rest. (3:20-21, 23, 26)

The arrows of Shaddai stick fast in me,
my spirit absorbs their poison,
God's terrors stand against me in array....
Oh may my prayer find fulfillment,
may God grant me my hope!
May it please God to crush me,
to give his hand free play and do away with
    me. (6:4, 8-9)

If I say, "My bed will comfort me,
my couch will soothe my pain,"
you frighten me with dreams
and terrify me with visions.
Strangling I would welcome rather,
and death itself, than these my sufferings.
I waste away, my life is not unending;
leave me then, for my days are but a breath.
    (7:13-16)

What is man that you should examine him,
subjecting him to your scrutiny,
that morning after morning you should
    examine him
and at every instant test him?
Will you never take your eyes off me
long enough for me to swallow my spittle?
    (7:17-19)

If he deigned to answer my citation,
could I be sure that he listened to my voice?
He, who for one hair crushes me,
who, for no reason, wounds and wounds
    again,
leaving me not a moment to draw breath,
with so much bitterness he fills me....
It is all one, and this I dare to say:
innocent and guilty, he destroys all alike.
When a sudden deadly scourge descends,
he laughs at the plight of the innocent.
When a country falls into a tyrant's hand,
it is he who blindfolds the judges.
Or if not he, who else? (9:16-18, 22-24)

Your own hands shaped me, modelled me;
and would you now have second thoughts,
    and destroy me?
You modelled me, remember, as clay is
    modelled,
and would you reduce me now to dust?...
And if I make a stand, like a lion you hunt
    me down,
adding to the tale of your triumphs.
You attack, and attack me again,
with stroke on stroke of your fury,
relentlessly your fresh troops assail me.
    (10:8-9, 16-17)

The passages quoted are sufficient to describe
Job's behavior. You can check for yourself those
that are missing.

24

I do not intend to analyze the totality of Job's message, but only what is useful for our purposes.

Job Says What He Has To Say

He never softens the truth. No artifice of rhetoric hides the depth of his grief or the power of his protest. He chooses impressively powerful words and images.

If I am tortured by revolt, resentment, anger—and even hatred, I might add—praying with Job teaches me that I may and must express these feelings to the Father. I learn that I should tell him everything, above all the thoughts and feelings directed at him, my God.

Because of his misfortunes, Job has no other channel open for communication with his God. He accepts the one he has and uses it.

While reading his accusations, we never feel that he is cut off from God, separated from his love. We discover the opposite, in fact. The farther we read, the less we understand—but the surer we are that God will not let things go on as they are. We believe that God will act on behalf of his faithful one. But after so many reproaches, accusations and demands, however, we cannot anticipate God's answer.

Since such tension would have been unbearable and would probably have scandalized some, the book's author was careful from the start to tell us that Job was perfect in God's eyes and was only being tested. But the trial, for it is a trial, is constructed in such a way as to make us understand that God is with Job, the just one, not only in spite of his words, but also *because of his words*. In fact, Yahweh finally says to Job's friends, "I will listen to him with favor and excuse your folly in not speaking of me properly as my servant Job has done" (42:8). "As my servant has done"? Why? If Job is so daring, it is precisely because he dares to believe that God will recognize his rights.

Put me right, and I will say no more;
show me where I have been at fault. (6:24)

And if I am guilty,
why should I put myself to useless
    trouble?...
Nonetheless, I shall speak, not fearing him:
I do not see myself like that at all. (9:29, 35)
But my words are intended for Shaddai;
I mean to remonstrate with God. (13:3)
Then arraign me, and I will reply;
or rather, I will speak and you shall answer
    me. (13:22)
Henceforth I have a witness in heaven,
my defender is there in the height.
My own lament is my advocate with God,
while my tears flow before him.
Let this plead for me as I stand before God,
as a man will plead for his fellows. (16:19-21)

If only I knew how to reach him,
or how to travel to his dwelling!
I would set out my case to him,
my mouth would not want for arguments....
He would see he was contending with an
   honest man,
and I should surely win my case. (23:3-4, 7)

If he weighs me on honest scales,
being God, he cannot fail to see my innocence.
   (31:6)

Job dares to believe that God is unfailing love. His conviction is summed up in his famous and beautiful words:

This I know: that my Avenger lives,
and he, the Last, will take his stand on earth.
After my awaking, he will set me close to
   him,
and from my flesh I shall look on God.
He whom I shall see will take my part:
these eyes will gaze on him and find him not
   aloof. (19:25-27)

Job as the Perfect Just Man

Job was introduced as the perfect just man: "Did you notice my servant Job? There is no one like him on the earth: a sound and honest man who fears God and shuns evil," said Yahweh to Satan (1:8). This perfect man acted in the way we have just examined! Fortified by our religious training and education, we might have been tempted to say, "Impossible!" We often consider it bad to become angry or to hate, think that it is even worse to express such feelings, and that it would be blasphemy to tell them to the Lord! And imagine the Lord being the target!

We forget how Moses talked to Yahweh. "Why do you treat your servant so badly?" he demanded on one occasion. "Why have I not found favor with you, so that you load on me the weight of all this nation? Was it I who conceived all this people, was it I who gave them birth? If this is how you want to deal with me, I would rather you killed me! If only I had found favor in your eyes, and not lived to see such misery as this!" (Num. 11:11, 12, 15).

Or maybe we forget the questioning of Gideon: "Forgive me, my lord, but if Yahweh is with us, then why is it that all this is happening to us now? And where are all the wonders our ancestors tell us of when they say, 'Did not Yahweh bring us out of Egypt?' But now Yahweh has deserted us; he has abandoned us to Midian" (Judges 6:13).

We forget that Scripture includes texts such as these *as prayers*—prayers we must not too quickly "spiritualize."

God, break their teeth in their mouths,
Yahweh, wrench out the fangs of these savage
lions!

May they drain away like water running to
   waste,
may they wither like trodden grass,
like a slug that melts as it moves,
like an abortion, denied the light of day.

Before they sprout thorns like the bramble,
green or scorched, may the wrath whirl them
   away!
What Joy for the virtuous, seeing this
   vengeance,
bathing their feet in the blood of the wicked!
"So," people will say, "the virtuous do have
   their harvest;
so there is a God who dispenses justice on
   earth!" (Ps. 58:6-11)

Slaughter them, God, before my people
   forget!
Harry them with your power and strike them
   down,
Lord, our shield! (Ps. 59:11)

May we soon see the pagans learning what
   vengeance
you exact for your servants' blood shed
   here!...
Pay our neighbors sevenfold, strike to the
   heart
for the monstrous insult proferred to you,
   Lord!

As we your people, the flock that you
  pasture,
giving you everlasting thanks,
will recite your praises forever and ever. (Ps.
  79:10, 12-13)

Treat them like Midian and Sisera,
like Jabin at the river Kishon,
wiped out at En-dor,
they served to dung the ground....
My God, bowl them along like tumbleweed,
like chaff at the mercy of the wind;
as fire devours the forest,
as the flame licks up the mountains,
drive them on with your whirlwind,
rout them with your tornado;
cover their face with shame,
until they seek your name, Yahweh.
Shame and panic be always theirs,
disgrace and death; and let them know this:
you alone bear the name Yahweh,
Most High over the whole world. (Ps.
  83:9-10, 13-18)

Do we know these prayers?

Let his life be cut short,
let someone else take his office;
may his children be orphaned
and his wife widowed!

May his children be homeless vagabonds,
beggared and hounded from their hovels;
may the creditor seize his possessions
and foreigners swallow his profits!

May no one be left to show him kindness,
may no one look after his orphans,
may his family die out,
its name disappear in one generation. (Ps.
109:8-13)

Destructive Daughter of Babel,
a blessing on the man who treats you
as you have treated us,
a blessing on him who takes and dashes
your babies against the rock! (Ps. 137:8-9)

I could enumerate the usual reactions to this
kind of behavior. We think such people are wrong,
almost unforgivably wrong! In reality this reaction
of ours is like that of Job's friends in that it does not
easily understand the prayers of God's people.

This is why we almost feel ourselves guilty
when we experience feelings like these, with no one
to point out an escape from this vicious circle.

We are devoured by the cancer of rebellion,
resentment, anger or hatred. As if that were not
enough, we add another burden to our misery: a
feeling of guilt.

So often we have been told, on the social plane
as well as the religious, that it is very serious to

31

have such feelings against ourselves, against others or against God. Since childhood we have been judged and condemned by the attitude of others until we now do the same thing to ourselves. And if God has been presented to us as the Supreme Judge as well, where can we go, to whom can we turn? We cannot keep from feeling anger or hatred; the fact that we feel them makes us feel guilty: we condemn ourselves, other people and God condemns us! We reach a dead end and turn ceaselessly around in circles, caught between the feelings that are consuming us and the guilt that is crushing us.

To whom can we go? To whom can we speak? What a relief it is to find a person who can accept us.

I can still hear the retreatant repeating three times before me, "God, I hate you because you let this happen." I still see her letting go of her tension because I did not pronounce any judgment, because the sky did not fall suddenly on her head.

When it is possible to speak a word, it liberates. We do not always remember that it is precisely a word, a Word articulated in our flesh, which has liberated us.

I think it is very consoling for us that Job was the perfect just man. In a sense he had no excuse for acting as he did; he was perfect. If the perfect just one of the Old Testament could behave so, *how much more can we*—we who are certainly not so perfect and just. Our weakness gives us the right to follow Job and to go even farther than he did, to express *everything, absolutely everything.* Job went to the limit of the violence possible for a just man. We can express the violence of an imperfect people. The important thing is always, for us as for Job, *to say what we have to say.* If God accepted a contest with the just and perfect Job *how much more easily will he accept one with us,* who are so poor and weak?

Job's innocence gave him the right to speak with such daring. We certainly do not have this right—we who are sinners. But we have the right conferred on us by our weakness...and our weakness should render us able to speak to God with daring, for Love is vulnerable to weakness.

If we cannot tell everything to our best friend—Abba, our Father in heaven—to whom can we tell it? *Absolutely nobody.* We would be totally lost in our feelings. But our Father loves us so much that he never wants us to be lost (see Luke 15).

I do not know if the Lord agreed with everything Job said. Neither do I know if Yahweh agreed with the prayers of his people when they prayed for the destruction of the babies of Babylon.

Is our conscience so delicate today, is our society so good, so devoid of violence and injustice, that we do not like to pray with such words—except when we pray for victory in a war that should give at least some difficulty to our enemies? For example, in some books of prayer passages I have just quoted have been suppressed because of so-called scruples of conscience. But what people feel has not been suppressed, and they find it difficult to realize that everything they feel can be expressed before God.

Probably the most important thing was for the words to be said, for the Jews to express absolutely everything to Yahweh.

Do we really believe that our Lord—Love, according to John's epistle—is so great that he is able to *listen to* all our prayers? Fortunately, some Christians are simple enough, deep enough, to understand this. The main question in my prayer life is not whether I am right or wrong, whether my words are good or bad. It is simply whether I love my Father enough to tell him everything in my heart, whether I believe in the immensity of a love which can understand and welcome any expression of my sorrow.

The Jews who dared to use such harsh words as prayers teach us that we do not love enough, that we do not believe enough that our Father is an astounding Love.

The Real Job: Jesus Christ

In reading these pages, some of you may still
doubt the truth of what they contain. So let us go to
the one prefigured by Job: Jesus himself, Jesus crying out from his cross, "My God, my God, why
have you forsaken me?" (Mark 15:34 and Ps. 22).

We are so accustomed to the Gospels that we
do not realize the importance of this question. The
Son of God himself is questioning the Father:
"Why?" No one dares imagine Jesus in the grip of
anger or hatred toward his Father. But he who was
the Just One par excellence dares to question God.
If Jesus in all his perfection had the audacity to ask
his Father "Why?" we can express to God *all our
whys*, since the why of the Son *of Man* embraced
ours. None of our whys can be excluded from his,
because all our whys are healed through his. Our
whys of anger and hatred are those that most need
to be saved. Job dared; Jesus dared; we have to
dare as well. And our weakness gives us an added
right and duty to cry out all our whys when we are
nailed to the cross.

The Father's Rebellion

More fascinating still, the why of Jesus was and
is the why of God himself. Is he not the Son *of God?*

35

Here we are confronted with a great mystery. Sometimes our words of revolt are the expression of God's "revolt" through us. As sons and daughters *of God*, we sometimes give expression to the groanings of the Spirit. Can we imagine the Father indifferent to the death of his own Son on the cross? Through the question of the crucified one we can often hear the Father questioning us: "Why did you act in that way? My people, why did you forsake me?" Through rebellious and suffering people, the Father questions all of us today.

"Why, my people, do you kill the innocent in war? Why do you produce and consume so much alcohol? Why do you build dams so fragile? Why do you work for profit and forget your employees? Why do you exploit developing nations? Why?"

"Why, my people, do you distort my creation through sin?"

So sometimes our revolt expresses the Father's own revolt rather than human rebellion against him. We think we are accusing him, while in reality he is sorrowfully questioning the world through us!

With two friends of mine I discovered this mysterious communion with the Father. They were parents of a son killed in a senseless accident. When I visited them, I listened to the rebellion of the mother. Her husband was trying to get her to be resigned, recalling her Christian faith.

At first I admired the husband's faith. It was difficult for me to accept the revolt of the wife; I thought her faith was weak.

But as the encounter went on, I slowly perceived a change in my thoughts and feelings until I said to myself: the Lord is certainly as saddened as she is right now; how could he accept such an accident caused by negligence and imprudence? And all of a sudden I understood that she was for us a witness to the sorrow of God. This was affirmed for me when I saw her engulfed in profound peace as I said to her, "Do not accuse the Lord; he is probably thinking the same thing you are. Do not think you are against him; he is beside you, speaking through you. Our Father has also 'lost' a child."

When we are faced with such situations, we can join our voices with Christ's and express our whys to God and man more openly.

Belief in the Father's Love

If Job dared to talk as he did, it was because he believed in Yahweh's justice and love. Christ also believed—perfectly. He kept repeating, "*My* God, *my* God...." Even in the depth of the terrible trial he went through, he affirmed the Lord as *his* God. Other words of his show us that he always believed his Father would re-establish justice, would remain with him. He said, for instance, "And yet I am not alone, because the Father is with me" (John 16:32). This was at the very beginning of his passion.

Jesus dared to ask "Why?" because he was sure of the Father's faithfulness. And the Father always was faithful.

I must explain an expression I have used: the "revolt" of the Father. A look at our own revolt will help us to understand the Father's.

Our revolt can go in one of two directions.

It can be translated into destructive words and actions. It can reach the point of feeling toward things, toward others, toward ourselves, a nihilistic attitude aimed at reducing these objects to nothingness. Consider the frustrated child who breaks everything, even what he has just built; consider extremist groups that destroy and kill without mercy; consider people who commit suicide.

But revolt can also invest its energy in reform, reconstruction, new creation. We could compile a long list of creative people on the social, political, cultural or religious plane who set out from a position of revolt. They revolted against a state which involved themselves and others and which became intolerable.

Creative Revolt

If destructive revolt is despair, creative revolt is hope.

The first aims at reducing everything to nothingness with the vague hope that something will be reborn from nothing; the second believes newness possible, since its creativity immediately sets it in motion in a visible manner. The God who created life from nothing is always ready to re-create, for he cannot and will not deny his creation. He promised

Noah, "I establish my Covenant with you: no thing of flesh shall be swept away again by the waters of the flood. There shall be no flood to destroy the earth again" (Gen. 9:11). And though he becomes angry with the Jews for adoring the golden calf, he commits himself to another beginning with Moses: "Leave me, now, my wrath shall blaze out against them and devour them; of you, however, I will make a great nation" (Ex. 32:10).

God can hope for everything from everything because his love can do everything. Since Jesus Christ, we know that he is not only the love "strong as death" in the Song of Songs (8:6), but a Love *stronger* than any death. The Father in his love has done everything to re-establish truth and the rights of his son: he has transformed the murder of Jesus into his glorification, into the source of grace for humanity.

The Father's reaction, then, can be pictured as, "What can I do with this? What can I *create* or *re-create with it*? What life can I extract from it for my Son, for all my sons and daughters?" The Father's "revolt" is a creative one, an inventive one, because Love is always creative and inventive for the good of the beloved. "We know that by turning everything to their good God cooperates with all those who love him, with all those that he has called according to his purpose," says Paul (Rom. 8:28). This is how the Father acted during the Passion of His Son.

For me this is the Father's revolt carried to its

final consequence. If Christ dared to ask "Why?" it was because of his perfect love for his Father and his perfect faith in the welcoming and transforming power of his love. We do not know if Jesus prayed all of Psalm 22 on the cross; but we can be sure that he knew the verses following "My God, my God, why have you deserted me?" Here are a few of them:

> For he has not despised
> or disdained the poor man in his poverty,
> has not hidden his face from him,
> but has answered him when called.
> The poor will receive as much as they want
> to eat.
> And my soul will live for him, my children
> will serve him;
> men will proclaim the Lord to generations
> still to come,
> his righteousness to a people yet unborn.
> All this he has done. (Ps. 22:24, 26, 30, 31)

Better still: After saying, "You never answer" (22:2)—which sums up well the psalm's plaint—the text in some versions abruptly affirms, "You have answered me" (22:21). At this point the psalmist invites the "brothers," the "assembly," even the "whole earth" to praise the Lord. Whether this break represents an act of hope or a reality already accomplished, in any case the thanksgiving which follows expresses absolute certitude about God's action: God is or will be faithful in working for his suffering servant. He will act in so striking a way that the psalmist going through the ordeal can *already* invite the whole earth to celebrate God and can affirm that "the poor will receive as much as they want to eat" (22:26).

This is probably why, filled with the confidence expressed in these verses, Jesus committed everything to his Father when everything was "accomplished" on the cross. Only the night before, he had asserted, "All I have is yours," in the certitude that "All you have is mine" (John 17:10).

The reflections of the foregoing pages show us how to act before the Lord when we are overwhelmed with suffering.

If All I Have
Is Really Yours, Father...

The first step is to be honest with ourselves and with the Lord when we suffer.

This means calling the feelings we know by their correct names. I must face myself as I am. If I am angry, I must recognize this. If I hate, I must not hide what I feel from myself or the Father and call it by some nice name. If it is hate, it is hate. To hide the reality of this fact is to lie.

To know what is going on in me always makes me feel better. An intelligent explanation of the life developing in us calmed our fears as adolescents. A sensitive and discerning announcement of approaching death has often given peace to gravely ill persons. Lies, on the contrary, achieve nothing.

The Father knows very well when I feel hatred because he sees the depth of my heart. Realizing that he knows it, I can more easily admit it. I have no reason to deny it.

Why must I refuse to deny it?

Because if I hide the truth, I risk closing the doors of my openness. When I need a doctor's care, I show him my wounds. I do not hide them and show him only what is healthy. Refusing to call hatred and resentment by their real names would be

43

hiding my wounds from the Lord. And if something has to be healed by him, it is precisely this kind of wound. The tumor must be made known; otherwise it may become malignant—a deadly cancer. "The man who lives by the truth comes out into the light," says John (3:21).

I may also block the only road of communication open to me right now with the Lord. This particular feeling pervades my whole life; everything is influenced by it. So it is probably the only springboard from which I can leap to the Lord. If I do not take advantage of it, I may lose the possibility of relating to him.

Theoretically speaking, it is probably not the best way; but concretely it is *my* way here and now. The problem is not to reject this way but to use it. Our Lord is realistic; he takes us as we are and where we are...and he can reach us anywhere. Do we not believe that "he descended into hell," meaning, according to one German theologian, that he can reach us anywhere since in sorrow no place exists that the Lord cannot now reach? And is not hatred a certain kind of "hell"? And did he not promise to be with us "all ways"? (Matthew 28:20)

The Nearness of the Lord

The next step is to see if my reaction is promoted by the Spirit within me—a reaction against the violation of peace or of justice, for example.

44

It is not always easy to discern this, but I have known persons who quickly realized that the Lord was beside them, "groaning" in them (Ro. 8:25). Immediately they were conscious of his closeness in prayer. Almost in the twinkling of an eye they saw the One they were accusing become their partner in sorrow. They discovered that they were sharing the Father's suffering before all the evil created by his sons and daughters. Mysteriously they were invited to enter into his compassion and mercy for sinful mankind.

I have known mothers and fathers who found this a royal road to the Lord—better than the path of false resignation or praise often counseled by indifferent preachers. Some of them found themselves impelled by the Spirit to do as the Father always does: to transfigure wounds, to re-create life from death.

Each of the three couples I knew had a mongoloid child. One couple even had two. I shall not describe the grief that accompanied the births in these three families. But I recall the question of one of the mothers when I went to visit her in the hospital and looked into the nursery: "Father, don't you notice anything?" Now they are all leaders in centers for handicapped children.

Sometimes my sufferings are such that I cannot act in this way. In that case I must try not to keep my words bottled up inside me.

I do not analyze myself, asking, "Am I right or wrong to be possessed by such feelings? Is this resentment, anger, hatred, good or bad? Did things

45

happen as I think or am I imagining them?" These questions may only build up guilt that judges and condemns me, adding another burden to the first. These questions especially risk trapping me in a web of muteness, the most dangerous dead-end in the spiritual life. Whether good or bad, right or wrong, these feelings are mine; the question is, "What can I do with them?"

Giving All to the Father

If I really believe that "All I have is yours," if my faith makes Jesus' words mine as a son or daughter of the same Father, *I have to give over to the Lord all that I have, including my feelings as they are now* and not as I would like them to be. The bread we offer is always poor, but as soon as it is offered to the Father and grasped by his Word it becomes the Eucharistic body of Jesus.

So not only must I express myself as I feel, but I have to offer myself. The simple fact that I am expressing myself is already an offering, but I can try to make a conscious gift of all my feelings. "Take, Lord: this is my body right now; this is my blood right now. I have at this moment no other body and blood to offer you. At least they are really yours." This brings to mind the prayer-poem of Dietrich Bonhoeffer in prison: "Whoever I am, Lord, you know I am yours."

I can say to the Father, "Remember Job; remember most of all your son Jesus. Although they were perfect, they dared to say, 'Why?' Remember me, this weak child of yours, and let me ask you 'Why?' let me tell you everything. If you allowed this to them as perfect men, how could you do otherwise for an imperfect person?

"Father, when I suffer I cannot help crying out, questioning, asking a thousand whys, like a child without self-control or understanding. I am sure you listen to me as a father patiently and lovingly listens to his child. You do much more, because you are *the Father* 'from whom every fatherhood...takes its name' (Eph. 3:14). So I am giving you all of this: my revolt, my resentment, my hatred, even though they are directed at you. To an observer it would seem that you were the target; but in reality you are the one whose hands are open to receive my gifts, all my gifts, and ready to tend to them because they are my wounds.

"Yes, my Father, our Father, *all* I have is really yours."

So in order to say truly, "Take, Lord," we express all our feelings to him. We tell him the whole story without changing a single word of the phrases exploding in our hearts. With him we can name people, places, times. Why mince words with my Father? "The Father already loves you," asserted Jesus (John 16:27). So I talk with him as I would with my closest friend.

47

This kind of praying will reveal the extent of our faith and hope in his love for us. Sometimes we will be aware of this faith and hope. Whether we are or not does not matter much, for the most important thing in loving is to act in accordance with love. This will signify our belief that he can see the depth of our wounds beneath the harshness of our expression, that his fantastic love can accept without judgment or condemnation his child who has been hurt so badly, that he can work with that hurt as he did with the murder of his Son, that he can produce grace from such poor bread.

Perhaps we shall even be able to believe that *he is already transforming our gift*, "transsubstantiating" our bread and wine. For he does not delay in transforming what we have and who we are.

Our Most Precious Treasure?

To give the Father all we have is to ask more or less consciously for the transformation of our poor bread.

Are resentment, disappointment, anger, hatred, really *poor* bread? I do not know.

The more I have dealt with people entering into the process described in this book, the more I have learned how difficult it was for them, at least in the beginning, to express their harshest feelings and give them to the Lord.

When we don't want to give something up, when we are reluctant to let go of it, it usually means that we are attached to it, treating it as a "treasure" we do not want to lose. Why are we so attached to it?

If it is a "treasure," it is often one we wish to hide from everybody, beginning with ourselves! If we are willing to reveal our sentiments to another, we are obliged to recognize them, to acknowledge them as ours; so we do not want this *revelation*. It is often a revelation that is very painful for us.

An "unknown" side of my being appears: If I am sometimes surprised by my irritation, how much more astonished am I at my anger! What panic takes hold of me when I discover that I am capable of hatred! After condemning the violence with which the news media constantly bombard us, I discover it in myself, crouched and ready to spring. I can no longer treat others like scapegoats and blame them for the world's violence. I myself am this violence.

"What? Me *too*?" we say to ourselves in amazement, seeing all the illusions we have about our righteousness fade away. It is hard to admit it to myself and others in the humility of truthfulness: "Yes, it is also part of *myself*."

Sometimes fear seizes hold of us in the face of this destructive power: "Will it be unleashed against another, against myself?

Taught never to hate, never even to say "I hate," one religious sister was crushed for weeks when she realized that she was capable of hatred.

Another example: I can still hear a convict, his wife's murderer, repeat to me: "I really don't know how I could have done it. I don't understand, I don't understand. . . .

During the war in Algeria, I was caught up in an unavoidable struggle. In order to protect fellow soldiers engaged in hand-to-hand combat, we had to open fire. I was astounded to discover in myself an extraordinary pleasure in chasing another man. Now when I read in the newspaper that two men started fighting over a parking place, how can I accuse them when I know what violence lies within myself?

But this violence has its origin in a basic aggressiveness that can be channeled in other directions. This was often brought out in the life of Jesus himself. Did he not chase the money-changers from the temple because the zeal for God's house had consumed him (John 2:13-22)? Did he not proclaim, "...the kingdom of heaven has been subjected to violence and the violent are taking it by storm" (Matt. 11:12)?

Instead of being frightened by this power, we can accept it as the energizing strength that makes sacrifice and martyrdom possible.

Giving Imperfect Gifts

Fear of looking ourselves in the eye can also have another origin.

Once during a retreat someone going through this kind of trial said to me, "It was difficult for me to give up to the Lord my anger and hatred because I wanted to *choose* the gift I would give the Lord. I was so happy and proud to offer my patience, my care for people, my love. I wanted to choose beautiful shoes in which to meet him. He showed me the kind of shoes that were for me: they were ugly and worn but they fitted my feet perfectly, so that I could walk and run toward him with ease. So I took *my* shoes, I gave *my* gifts; I gave over to him *my* anger and *my* hatred." We both knew that she was right.

So often we think that we will please the Lord with our best gifts—what *we* consider our best gifts. We forget that we are a sinful people, able to give only imperfect and ambiguous gifts. We forget that Jesus came among us to invite not virtuous people but sinners (Matt. 9:13) as the real Good Samaritan (Luke 10), filled with love and pity for sick people who need care. So our best gifts are our wounds, even though we do not understand this. The best gift we can give to a doctor passionately concerned with our health is to show him our wounds and give them over to his hands.

The Fear of Losing Ourselves

Sometimes we hold on to the "treasure" of our anger and hatred through a kind of masochism.

Strange though it may seem, an ache in my back, my leg, my stomach, no matter how painful, makes me aware of that part of my body and therefore of myself. I am not spontaneously aware of the parts of me that are not causing me pain.

Likewise, strong feelings of anger and hatred make me more conscious of my own reality, even of my own identity. And when I really detest someone, when I am deeply possessed by hatred, my identity is this "Pierre-who-hates."

I am therefore afraid that if I give up my hatred I will lose "Pierre" while losing the "one-who-hates." People who have been through this say, "I was afraid of being lost, of being totally empty, of being no longer myself."

We do not understand that the Father, even while seeing the Pierre who is full of hate, knows the loving Pierre. We do not believe that the Father loves this Pierre no matter what his feelings may be.

When we give him everything, we may feel lost, it is true—but we will be lost in his arms!

In fact, a morbid desire to be lost sometimes makes us hold on to our sentiments like a "treasure."

We are fascinated, as it were, by the destructive aspect of the force we feel in ourselves, hypnotized by the dizziness and annihilation it seems to promise. It seems that to disappear would be no more than to rest. A simple toothache can make us quickly desire to end it all; so let us not be surprised that a person who is suffering intensely dreams of suicide and takes pills intended to bring on sleep.

Job himself appeals several times to the sleep of death; we can re-read his words in the texts we have cited. He even aspires to the formless void which Sheol was for the Jews: "All I look forward to is dwelling in Sheol" (Job 17:13). At times there seems to be so little difference between a life of suffering and this colorless place: "For my soul is all troubled, my life is on the brink of Sheol; I am numbered among those who go down to the Pit, a man bereft of strength," says the author of Psalm 88 (3-4).

53

The chosen people needed centuries of hope before they could challenge this nothingness. Men and women cried out without ceasing:

So my heart exults, my very soul rejoices,
my body, too, will rest securely,
for you will not abandon my soul to Sheol,
nor allow the.one you love to see the Pit;
you will reveal the path of life to me,
give me unbounded joy in your presence,
and at your right hand everlasting pleasures.
    (Ps. 16:9-11)

It was only very late that the Jewish faith integrated the conviction that "Death was not God's doing, he takes no pleasure in the extinction of the living. To be—for this he created all" (Wisdom 1: 13-14). Finally, Jesus was needed to proclaim without reservation that God "is God, not of the dead, but of the living" (Mark 12:27).

At other times we hold on to our "treasure" because we like to see ourselves as victims.

Some people enjoy being victims because it gives them the right to prosecute the one they consider responsible. Through their attacks they try to force the "guilty" person to remain bound to them and to pay for his "crime." Sometimes victims become persecutors, using the power of revenge given them because of what happened.

To give up hatred is to give up this power over

the other, admitting that he is free to accept and build again reconciliation and love.

When we experience such feelings against the Lord, let us keep in mind that we cannot force him, that force is not necessary because he already loves us. There is no room for revenge against the Father because he never acts against us.

Finally, if we do not easily part with the "treasure" of our hatred and resentment, it is because we are afraid of losing everything.

Through hating the one involved, we think we have already lost his friendship or love. We were often told that it was wrong to feel that way toward God; as soon as we feel resentful we think he is far away from us.

But we are still communicating with the other, with the Lord, through feeling. A bond still exists between us. We are not sure that when we come back to our friend, our spouse, our Father, we will still have their love. Revenge could prompt them to refuse to love us again.

Unsure that love will be returned, ready to get rid of our hatred, we are terribly afraid to be left with nothing. If my friend, my spouse, my Father, does not go along with me, in the end I shall be *without love, without hate, without any communication or relationship*. With the other completely lost to me, I shall be all alone.

But we reduce the size of the Father's love to the loves we see around us. Let us at least remember the words of the Lord, "Does a woman forget her baby at the breast, or fail to cherish the son of her womb? Yet even if these forget, I will never forget you. See, I have branded you on the palms of my hands" (Isaiah 49:15:16).

Thus our resentment, anger and hatred are often a "treasure" we hold on to for many reasons. Though sometimes valid in dealing with people, they never are toward the Father who said, "Ephraim, how could I part with you? Israel, how could I give you up? My heart recoils from it, my whole being trembles at the thought. For I am God, not man" (Hosea 11:8-9).

So let us give up this illusory "treasure" to the Father and discover a real one.

We are a treasure. *We* are the Father's pearl. According to the parables of the treasure hidden in a field and of the pearl of great price (Matt. 13:44-46), did he not look for us, try to find us in whatever field we were hidden? Did he not sell everything he possessed to purchase us? Yes, he did; even to accepting his Son in our flesh, his Son crucified for us. (See Romans 5:1-11 and 8:31-39.)

We are this treasure, this pearl of great price, because the Father sees in each of us forever the unique son or daughter that we are, the unique face of his Son that we are.

May I Hate God?

When we can act as I have tried to describe throughout these pages, I think we will change our mind about the kind of hatred about which I have been speaking. That is why I put a question mark in the title.

Let us imagine someone praying, expressing to the Lord all his feelings—all of them without exception. He feels resentment, anger, even hatred. But if he prays like this, can we classify as hatred what he calls "hatred"? I am not so sure. Let me explain.

When people can express harsh feelings to the One or ones who are their object, love is *already* stronger in them than their feelings. Love is *already* transforming, transfiguring, this feeling into something else, something closer to love than to hatred. The power of the Resurrection is *already* at work in them. Perhaps there is hatred present as long as people are mute, absolutely mute; but as soon as they decide to express what is in their heart to the other, something is *already* changing and maybe even *already* changed.

As I have said, this expression is a desire for reconciliation. If I can tell you, my friend, that I hate you, and if you can accept my words and feelings, then Love is present, working and conquering. You are still alive and present in my life, even though in sorrow; I am coming back to you, and you are welcoming me.

When such things happen, I remember another line of Dietrich Bonhoeffer from the poem already quoted: "...Or does something in me, like a vanquished army, flee in disorder before a victory already won?"

How true all this is of the Lord; we are so much surer of him than of any other friend.

So let us go to our Father and say "Father, all I have is yours."

Soon he will reveal that he is saying the same words to us.

Appendix I

*How the Question Treated in This Book
Is Dealt With in Directed Retreats*

A directed retreat, to put it simply, is a retreat during which the retreatant encounters the retreat master for a short while each day in order to discern with him what the Lord is saying through the retreat process.

I would like to explain briefly how some of us who are retreat masters apply the results of this book.

When the retreatant begins to reveal in his notes or verbal comments a certain enduring anger, hatred or resentment aimed at people or at the Lord, the retreat master tries to discern whether or not it is possible for the retreatant to face this kind of feeling. If the answer is yes, the retreat master explains the whole process of what they must do together.

The retreat master asks the retreatant to read outside of prayer time the book of Job, especially the chapters in which Job speaks. Why?

First, to discover that we can express everything to the Lord as I have explained in this book. Second, to be helped by the words, thoughts and mood of Job himself. Job becomes a guide, companion and brother who supports the retreatant's undertaking.

Then the retreatant must write the words which come to his mind and heart exactly as if he were talking to the Lord, to the extent that this is possible. Writing down his thoughts allows the retreatant to make them more objective and to confront them in black and white. He writes *his own book of Job*.

After this the retreatant gives the notes to the retreat master to symbolize that all of this is no longer his but has been given over to the Lord. The retreat master reads them quickly and silently in the presence of the retreatant without any comment—certainly without judgement or condemnation, but also without approval. When he has finished, he gives the notes back to the retreatant.

Sometimes the process must be repeated several times. I do not think it should be necessary to do it too often; whenever I did it, it was twice at the most.

Explanations To Clarify Specific Points

—*Why do this outside of prayer time?*

It does not seem necessary to disturb, at least directly, what goes on during prayer. Often prayer during this process and following it gives information about the results on the spiritual level. For instance, if things are going well, the retreatant experiences peace more frequently and enduringly within himself.

—Why does the retreat master read the notes without comment?

His reading is a symbolic act which means for the retreatant that he has expressed and given up all that he felt. Comment would immediately destroy the purpose of the process, which is to understand that it is not a question of appreciating the value of the feelings, their rightness or wrongness, but of expressing them freely to our loving Father. How could a retreat master pronounce judgment about this kind of relationship with the Lord?

I suppose also that if the retreat master were to comment the retreatant might easily think, "He asked me to do that because he was looking for information about my life, about things I had not yet mentioned." The retreatant might then lose confidence in the retreat master.

—Why does the retreat master give the notes back to the retreatant?

First, because they are very personal and do not belong to him. Also, to symbolize that the Lord is giving back the gift—as a gift *from him* already changed and transformed. I have seen retreatants reread their notes after this process with a peace they never knew before; the past had been exorcised.

—Is there a risk of explosion?

I presume that the retreat master would think of that before doing anything. With an intelligent spiritual master I do not think that we need fear any kind of explosion. The directed retreat is a framework which allows the persons involved to channel the process more easily. It is probably better not to wait until the last day of the retreat to begin something like this, of course. The process has actually begun as soon as the retreatant starts to express to the retreat master the kind of feeling in question, even before the latter has suggested anything we have described. The method becomes a way to systematize the process if the retreat master feels that it should be undertaken. And, of course, I believe that the Lord is present, doing what he alone can do.

—Why does the retreat master describe the whole process before entering into it?

The retreatant has to know and to accept it freely. The process is not a trap; it brings about an openness into which love can enter for the purpose of healing.

Appendix II

*Some Useful Scripture Texts for Prayer
in Time of Suffering*

Here are some Scripture references for help in praying. It is not possible to comment on each of them, to add exegetical explanations, so they are simply indicated without comment.

Certainly they are numerous, but we must not narrow down the choice of those available to us. One text will "speak" to one person, and have nothing to "say" to another.

We have not singled out specific chapters or verses of the books of Job, Ecclesiastes or Lamentations, because in each case the entire book should be taken as a whole. Ecclesiastes may appeal to those who feel a kind of skepticism.

Neither have we cited texts on the Passion of Christ. When one is suffering, it is no doubt the whole of the Passion that is most suitable for prayer. We find it in the following chapters: Matthew 26 and 27; Mark 14 and 15; Luke 22 and 23; John 18 and 19.

Finally, the categories we have chosen are rather general. But one cannot classify or distinguish precisely all that comes into play in time of suffering. Under different headings will be found for instance texts that express suffering and texts that help in facing it.

ADVERSARIES: When our suffering comes from people who act as enemies, traitors, persecutors.

Old Testament

1 Samuel 17:40-51
2 Samuel 11:1-12:7
1 Kings 19:1-14
Tobit 3:1-6
Judith 9:1-14; 13:4-5
Esther 4:17a-17z (in the Greek)
2 Maccabees 6:18-31; 7:1-42
Psalms 3; 5; 7; 9-14; 17; 18; 21; 22; 25-28; 31;
    35-38; 41; 52-59; 62-64; 69-71; 73; 83; 101; 109;
    120; 140; 142-144
Wisdom 1-3; 5
Ecclesiasticus 12:8-18; 22:19-26; 28:13-26; 37:1-6
Isaiah 14:3-21
Jeremiah 1:17-19; 11:20; 12:1-3; 15:15b-18;
    17:14-18; 18:18-23; 20:7-18
Ezekiel 2:1-3:11; 34
Daniel 13

New Testament

Matthew 5:1-12; 10:17-25; 10:26-33; 13:53-58;
    16:21-23; 17:22-23; 20:17-19; 21:33-46; 23:1-39;
    24:9-13—and parallel texts in the other Gospels
Luke 4:16-30; 10: 17-20; 10:29-37
John 13

Acts 4:1-31; 5:21-33; 7; 9:1-19, 23-25; 12; 13:44-52;
  16:16-24; 17:1-15; 19:25-40; 21:27-40
Romans 12:14-21
Philippians 1:27-30
2 Timothy 3
1 Peter 3:13-17; 4:12-19
1 John 3:13

ASKING FOR GRACE: For oneself in suffering.

Old Testament
Genesis 15:1-21
Exodus 3:1-22; 33:18-23 and 34:5-9
1 Samuel 1:1-18
1 Kings 3:4-15
Esther 4:17a-17z (in the Greek)
Wisdom 9
Isaiah 55:1-3, 10-11; 58:6-12
Ezekiel 36; 37

New Testament
Matthew 12:38-42; 15:21-28; 16:1-4; 17:14-20;
  18:19-20—and parallel texts in the other Gospels
Luke 7:36-50; 11:5-13; 18:1-8
Acts 4:23-31
Romans 10:8
2 Corinthians 12: 7-10
Ephesians 3:14-20
1 John 5:14-15

DOUBT: When murmuring against God rises up
within us because of trial; when we doubt his

love, his faithfulness, his listening to us. These texts refer to the act of faith in him and can help us bear the trial of doubt.

Old Testament

Genesis 8:15-9:17
Exodus 3:1-22; 16:1-18; 17:1-7; 33:18-23 and 34:5-9
Deuteronomy 4:32-38; 7:7-16
Joshua 24:1-28
Judges 6:11-24
2 Samuel 7:18-29 (1 Chronicles 17:16-27)
Nehemiah 9:5-37
Psalms 4; 9; 10; 13; 16; 30; 31; 33; 34; 39; 40;
    42-44; 46; 51; 61; 103; 108; 136; 145; 146
Isaiah 32:15-20; 40:1-11; 42:14-17; 43:1-5; 44:1-5;
    46:1-4; 49:7-26; 54:1-17; 55:1-13; 60:1-22; 62:1-12
Ezekiel 34:17-31; 36; 37; 47:1-12
Daniel 3:8-24; 3:24a-90 (Greek text); 3:24-30
Hosea 2:16-25; 11:1-9; 14:2-9
Joel 2:12-27; 3
Amos 9:11-15
Jonah 2
Micah 6:8
Zephaniah 3:11-20
Haggai 2:1-9

New Testament

Matthew 9:10-13; 12:15-21; 18:12-14;
    21:18-22—and parallel texts in the other Gospels
Luke 1:67-79; 2:1-20, 29-32; 15:1-32; 19:1-10;
    24:13-35
John 3; 4; 9; 10; 14-17; 20-21

Acts 5:34-39
Romans 8; 10:8
Galatians 3:23-4:7
Ephesians 1:3-14; 2; 3:20-21
Hebrews 6:9-12;11
James 2:14-26
1 John 4:7-21
Revelation 21-22

TRIAL. Before, during and after trial in the most general sense of the term, whether personal or collective, due to the fault of others or of ourselves.

Old Testament

Exodus 3:1-22
1 Samuel 17:40-51
2 Samuel 22:1-51
1 Kings 3:4-15; 8:30-51 (2 Chronicles 6:21-39); 19:1-14
2 Kings 5:1-27
Tobit 3:11-17; 8:15-17; 11:14-15
Judith 16:1-17
Esther 4:17a-17z (Greek text)
1 Maccabees 2:49-70; 3:1-9
2 Maccabees 6:18-31; 7:1-42
Psalms 4; 6; 30-34; 39; 40; 42; 43; 46; 51; 61; 66; 77; 79; 80; 85; 86; 88; 90; 91; 94; 102; 107; 116; 118; 121; 123; 130; 136-138; 141
Song of Songs 2:8-14
Ecclesiasticus 36:1-17; 51:1-12
Isaiah 9:1-6; 32:15-20; 41:8-20; 43:1-5; 44:1-5;

46:1-4; 49:7-26; 52:13-53:12; 55:1-3;
Baruch 1:15-3:8; 4:5-5:9
Ezekiel 16; 34; 36; 37
Daniel 3:8-24; 3:24a-90 (Greek text); 3:24-30;
   6:17-29; 13
Joel 2:12-17
Jonah 2
Habakkuk 1:2-4; 1:12-2:3
Haggai 2:1-9

New Testament

Matthew 6:7-13,25-34; 7:7-11; 16:21-23; 20:20-23;
   28:1-8—and parallel texts in the other Gospels
Mark 12:41-44
Acts 27:9-44
Romans 13:11-14
1 Corinthians 4:9-13
2 Corinthians 2:14-17; 4:7-18; 6:1-10; 12:7-10
Ephesians 6:10-18
Philippians 3
2 Timothy 2:1-13
Hebrews 10:32-39; 12:1-4
James 1:2-12
1 Peter 4:12-19
Revelation 6:9-11; 7:9-17

TRIAL FROM GOD: When we feel that our trial
was sent by God.

Old Testament

Genesis 12:1-9; 15:1-21; 22:1-19; 32:23-33
Ruth 1:16-17; 3

1 Samuel 3:1-10
Psalms 13; 17; 22; 38; 44; 66; 74; 79; 80; 85; 88;
    89; 94; 102
Song of Songs 1:5-7; 2:8-14; 3:1-4
Isaiah 40:1-11; 49:7-26
Jeremiah 14:19-22; 30; 31; 33
Baruch 1:15-3:8; 4:5-5:9
Hosea 2:11-25

New Testament

Matthew 10:34-39 and parallel texts
Luke 1:26-38; 2:33-35; 2:41-52; 3:15-18
Hebrews 4:12-13; 10:5-7
James 1:13-18

EXHAUSTION: When we feel ourselves
exhausted by the trial we are undergoing.

Old Testament

Genesis 15:1-21
1 Kings 19:1-14
Psalms 28; 69; 88; 102; 130; 143
Haggai 2:1-9

New Testament

Luke 24: 13-35

BURDEN: When the trial is a burden too heavy
to bear; for instance, when we have to assume a
responsibility that seems overwhelming.

Old Testament

Genesis 32:23-33
Numbers 11:10-15
1 Samuel 17:40-51
1 Kings 3:14-15; 19:1-14
Isaiah 46:1-4
Haggai 2:1-9

New Testament

Matthew 5:1-12; 11:28-30 and parallel texts
Luke 5:1-11

INTERCESSION: When we wish to pray for someone undergoing a trial.

Old Testament

Genesis 18:16-33
Exodus 32:7-14, 30-32; 33:12-17
Numbers 14:10-19
Deuteronomy 9:25-29
Nehemiah 1:5-11

New Testament

Matthew 25:31-46

DEATH: When trial is death of any kind.

Old Testament

Genesis 4:1-16; 22:1-19; 32:23-33
2 Samuel 1:26; 19:1-5
1 Kings 19:1-14

Psalms 13; 16; 18; 30; 56; 88; 116; 118; 130
Wisdom 1:13-15
Ecclesiasticus 27:30-28:7; 38:16-23; 41:1-4
Isaiah 38:9-20
Jonah 2

New Testament

Matthew 9:18-26; 16:24-28; 17:1-8; 17:22-23;
   21:33-46; 22:23-33 and parallel texts in the other
   Gospels
Luke 7:11-17
John 6; 11
Acts 2:14-36; 5:17-21; 9:32-43; 12; 16:25-40;
   20:7-12, 17-38
1 Corinthians 15
Philippians 2:6-11
Colossians 3:1-3
1 Thessalonians 4:13-18
1 John 3:14-24

FORGIVENESS: When our trial demands
forgiveness either from us or from God; when we
know the joy of forgiveness—given to us or given
by us.

Old Testament

Genesis 9:9-17; 18: 16-33; 45: 1-14; 50:15-21
Exodus 23:1-9; 32:7-14, 30-32
Deuteronomy 4:29-40; 6: 14-25; 7:7-16; 10:12-22;
   30:1-20
1 Samuel 24:1-23; 26:1-25

2 Samuel 11:1—12:13

1 Kings 8:20-53 (2 Chronicles 6:21-42)

2 Kings 5:1-27

Nehemiah 9

Tobit 3:1-6; 13:1-17

Esther 14:17a-17z (Greek)

Psalms 1; 6; 32; 36-37; 44; 51; 78; 80; 85; 90-91;
    95; 102-103; 106; 112; 116; 119; 130; 133; 138-139;
    143

Proverbs 24:17-18

Wisdom 11:15—12:27

Sirach 15:11-20; 17:15-32; 21:1-3; 27:30—28:7

Isaiah 1:10-20; 3:16-24; 4:2-5; 5:1-7; 6:6-7; 9:1-6;
    11:1-5; 25:6-12; 30:19-26; 40:1-11; 41:17-20; 42:1-3;
    43:22-25; 44:21-22; 47:1-15; 49:7-26; 50:1-3;
    52:13—53:12; 54-55; 58:6-12; 59:1; 60-62

Jeremiah 3:1-5, 12-13; 7:21-28; 9:1-8, 12-15;
    15:10-21; 31; 33:6-16

Baruch 1:15—3:8; 4:5—5:9

Ezekiel 16; 18; 20; 36; 37:1-14; 43:1-9; 47:1-12

Daniel 9:24

Hosea 2:8-25; 6:1-6; 11:7-9; 14:2-9

Joel 1:13-20; 2:12-17; 3:1-5; 4:18-21

Amos 2:6-16; 5:4-6, 14-15, 21-27; 8:11-12; 9:11-15

Jonah 3

Micah 4:1-8; 7:18-20

Zephaniah 2:1-3; 3:9-20

Haggai 2:1-9

Zechariah 8; 9:9-17; 12:10—13:3

New Testament

Matthew 5:21-26, 38:48; 7:1-5; 9:1-8; 18:15-18;
   18:21-35; 22:34-40 and parallel texts in the other
   Gospels
Luke 15:1-32; 19:1-10
John 8:1-11
Romans 12:3-21; 13:8-10; 14:1-15; 15:7-13
1 Corinthians 12; 13
Ephesians 4:1-6, 25-32
Philippians 2:1-11
1 Timothy 1:12-17
Titus 3:4-7
Philemon in its entirety
1 Peter 3:8-12
1 John 1:9-11

FEAR: Resulting from the trial we foresee or
experience.

Old Testament

Genesis 22:1-19; 32:23-33
Exodus 14:10-18
Deuteronomy 7:17-24
Joshua 1:1-9
1 Samuel 17:40-51
1 Kings 19:1-14
2 Kings 5:1-27
Psalms 25; 27; 32; 33; 77; 86; 91; 102; 116; 118
Isaiah 41:8-20; 43:1-5; 44:1-5; 46:1-4

New Testament

Matthew 8:23-27; 14:22-33 and parallel texts in the
   other Gospels
Luke 5:1-11
Romans 8:31-39
Ephesians 6:10-18

SUFFERING: When trial appears as sickness,
physical illness in particular.

Old Testament

Exodus 3:1-22
2 Kings 20:1-6
Isaiah 38:9-20
Psalms—see *TRIAL*

New Testament

Matthew 8:1-15; 9:27-34; 15:29-31; 20:29-34 and
   parallel texts in the other Gospels
Mark 7:31-37; 8:22-26
Luke 13:10-17; 14:1-6; 17:11-19
John 5:1-18
Acts 3:1-10
Colossians 3:24
2 Timothy 2:1-13
Hebrews 5:7-8

TEMPTATION: When trial takes the form of
temptation.

Old Testament

Genesis 3; 4:1-16
Exodus 33:18-23; 34:5-9
Joshua 24:1-28
Tobit 8:5-8
Psalms 15; 19; 32; 37; 49-52; 73; 81; 95; 119; 141

New Testament

Matthew 4:1-11; 12:43-45; 15:10-20; 18:8-10 and
   parallel texts in the other Gospels
Luke 12:35-48; 14:15-24, 28-33
Romans 7:14-25
2 Corinthians 12:7-10
Galatians 5:13-15
2 Timothy 4:1-5
Hebrews 12:1-4
James 1:13-18; 2:1-13; 3; 4; 5:1-6

TEMPTATION: To let everything go.

Old Testament

Genesis 8:15-9:17
Joshua 24:1-28
Ruth 1:16-17; 3
Haggai 2:1-9
Psalms—see *TEMPTATION* above

New Testament

Hebrews 12:1-4

VENGEANCE: When we have the desire to avenge ourselves.

Old Testament

Genesis 4:1-16
1 Samuel 24:1-23; 26:1-25
Psalms—see *ADVERSARIES*
Wisdom 2:10-20
Ecclesiasticus 27:30-28:7
Jeremiah 10:23-25; 11:20 and 12:1-3; 17:14-18; 18:18-23; 20:7-18
Ezekiel 34
Joel 4:18-21
Obadiah 16-21
Habakkuk 3

New Testament

Matthew 5:21-26; 38-48; 7:1-5, 12 and parallel texts in the other Gospels
Luke 6:27-38; 9:51-56